ASHES IN THE DAWN

Collected Poems

To Lily Lou + Buckskin Bob

Glenn Knight

GLENN KNIGHT

2006

Copyright © 2005 by Glenn Knight

ISBN 0-7414-2588-2

Published by:

INFINITY
PUBLISHING.COM

1094 New DeHaven Street, Suite 100
West Conshohocken, PA 19428-2713
Info@buybooksontheweb.com
www.buybooksontheweb.com
Toll-free (877) BUY BOOK
Local Phone (610) 941-9999
Fax (610) 941-9959

Printed in the United States of America

Printed on Recycled Paper

Published June 2005

To the great poets whom I have read and loved
these many years

I

Brush the ashes from the coals at dawn.
We had thought to burn all our dreams away,
But there may rise new dreams from
Ashes in the dawn.

Lay the laurel twig upon the coals
Lying there beneath the ashes,
Stored away for another day.
How then may we discover

Why it is that dreams burn away
Only to have more dreams arise?
Watch the smoke rise from new laid
Twigs and branches

Grown from still living trees.
Shall we go again into that land
Where dreams are yet to grow?
Ah, yes! We'll go there again.

Brush the ashes from the coals at dawn.
Let us burn new dreams this day.

II

Come, let us borrow
        now
from some far tomorrow
        balm
from sweet scented yarrow
        to
ease the pain of this day's sorrow.

Diana, did you stop for me today
        as
you made your wandering way
        home
while westering sun's warm fingers lay
        a
soft caress on yonder tree this late in May?

There along the way stands a deer
        who
might have walked here
        where
I stand in grass not yet growing sere
        though
time will change it all, I fear.

Come. Let us look
        at
this cool running brook
        where
fish swim in yon secluded nook
        though
I have neither line nor hook.

I do not talk with time that rolls
        along
blue earth dream, turning souls
        toward
this stream where willows weep for rolls
        of
men and women lost in fields of fallow folds.

III

Do I dare to dream again
      though
soon moon's shadow comes anon
      where
dreams are laid in dust in some far glen
      though
we be idle flesh both now and then.

Pluck the lyre, sing the song
      and
perhaps some day I'll come along
      and
hear the bell's deep ringing gong
      though
'tis not heaven's gate where I belong.

Let us remember these days
When time has flown.
Let us remember these ways
When soft winds have blown
Soft green grass and drifting sand
To tell us still that life is grand.
Yes!

Let us remember these days
For they do not come always
To light our lives.
Full ripe the bees' hives!
Yes!

V

Come, walk with me beside the sea
Where soundless breakers roam
And pebbles rise at dawn.

We'll taste the wind that slides along
And ripples marsh where water lilies grow
And bends dune grass growing row on row.

We'll hear the fish at school
In fathomed waters where no waves break.
*(Do they learn there what rules the sea can
        bear?)*

We'll smell the gull's clear cry
Break 'gainst shore pine's rising arms
In wonder at a gray, gray sky.

We'll feel footsteps beneath our feet
From those who've gone before, footsteps
lying deep
  'Neath ribboned sand raised by wind's silent
        roar.

We'll see what passed before
And know what and when and where.
Sea shells speak of this and more.

So, come walk and talk with me
Beside the sea while crimson skies
Deny the day that came before,

For God nor I can reason why
No blessings come our way.
Yet flat smooth stone can skip away

'Cross dying wave slipping back
To foam once more
Where still waters tumble o'er and o'er.

My Lord, speak soft within my soul
Now filled with lead, not gold.
For such is life when love has flown, or so
I'm told.

VI

Little Bird, I loved to see you so—
    Yellow, black and silver,
        Sitting on my fountain stone—

That stone bored through by man
    And tubed in black to black pump
        That made the water flow.

Yellow bird with wings of black
    And silver, did you know
        That water where you dipped

Your beak and spread your wings
    Was the last you would know?
        But then, how could you
          know?

I did not see him lying there
    Beneath the bench where on I sat—
        Long, sinuous, black. Quiet he
          lay,

Unmoving, ebony carved, surreal—
    As I have often seen him before—
        Sapphire eyes aglow and
          twitching tail.

Black Cat, I saw you there—
    Yellow bird with black and silver
        wing
        In mouth—saw you spring
          across the lawn.

Little Bird, will you come again
    In some now unknown hereafter
        And sit upon my shoulder

And speak of things that I should know,
    Of water cool upon grey stone,
        Of flying high through air and
        wind,

Of life too short to know at all
    The melody your sweet song calls,
        The swift dart of some black
        cat?

Si pecasse negamus, fallimur,
Et nulla est in nobis veritas;
Exhoereditare filium non potest pater nisi.
O lenti, lenti, currita noctis equi.

We are astonished by your brown study;
Your clothes so trimly cut
Are blue, yellow, red, and gay.
We could not dream you live in hate all day.

Your voice is mild, your words distinct;
"In this urn lies dead Orestes' ash," you say.
And I believe Orestes dead;
I put away my dread.

"Is Agamemnon dead?" you ask,
"Is Orestes' father dead?"
I give you back the answer, "Yes.
How did you come to guess."

"In Coatesville, Korea, Birmingham, and
        Hue,
I saw him fall. I guessed then," you say,
"That he was doomed as are they all
Who drink of vinegar and gall."

You ask, "His mother, does she lie there
In white Aegosthos' bed?"
I cannot answer that;
I tremble; my voice falls flat.

"And does dark Electra, brooding, mourn
Her dead father,
Or does the white seducer lay
False words and lead her in his way?"

And now the mask is stripped away;
You smile, but in your eyes, Orestes eyes,
There is unveiled for all to see
What lies in store for mine— and for me.

You say, "The ash this urn holds
Is the ash of the thousand lies you've told.
I've come to claim the debt at last
That I have earned from your dead past."

And now we are astonished by your brown
          study;
That stern visage will not turn
From its set way. The years of hating hate
Have come to us too late.

You say, "You had your chance
To right a wrong;
Now live the world you have made
And pay the debt you have not paid."

Black Orestes, I cannot plea
For pity, compassion, mercy,
For all that I would say
Is but an echo of the song you sang all day.

The gates shall open soon, the palace gates,
And shall the bodies lie in piles,
Mute, desolate testimony
Of our failed patrimony?

"No father may disinherit his son," you say.
And when you have slain all you can slay,
When all your rampant hearts are done,
What, then, Orestes, will you give *your* son?

He who says he is without sin deceives
            himself;
There is no truth in him.
Nor may the father disinherit the son.
Run slowly, slowly, horses of the setting sun.

O lente, lente, currite noctis equi:
"Run slowly, slowly, steeds of the night."
While dark Orestes ponders freedom's plight;
Consummatum est turns out the light.

VIII

Carved stone, speak to me!
Tell me things I should have known.
Tell what you know of life—
Those tales, those trails, those things lost by
       the way.
Tell me truths the earth laid down
In time now lost, run wild with beast, bird and
       fish.
In your heart, not warm at all as is your stone
       skin,
Lie those truths bound by cords that will not
       break
For will or want or God's own sake.
Your glyphs start the tale, but they lie on your
       stone skin,
Carved and drawn there in a time
when men passed this way and made
Their marks—we can't tell when or why.

Why these circles here?
Why this snaking line?
Do they tell of life once lived
When you came here to gather seed
Or other things to eat?
Perhaps they show a path where we should
       go?
There is a man, I know, but what man is he
Who stands so? Come. Let me know!

Come stone, speak.
Give me truths grown old, out of use.
Place your tales in my heart and let me pen
       them, one by one.
Let the night come and go.

Let the stars shine, let the moon shine,
Let the sun shine down!
Tell me true all you've known.
I'd like that.

In the early fall, the fog drifts in from a western sea,
Climbs the shoulders of the mountains along the
       shore,
Slips down their slopes and glides
Along the hills that border the valley,
Then slides slowly out over the valley and covers the
       sun.

In the late fall, the rains come to Oregon.
Leaves drift in the wind and branches of trees
Stand black against a gray sky;
And the rain, the silver rain, falls gently on the land.
The rains come to Oregon in the late fall.

The sky is gray and damp through long winters.
Sometimes snow comes and the land lies white and
       long.
Then the trees and brush trace their strange geometry
Against a brighter cloth. And when the cold clamps
       down
Hard upon the land, what sun comes through is thin
       and long
And casts black shadows on the ground.

In the early spring, the land is touched with green
Which grows and spreads until the land leaps
With green and green and green. There is the green,
The emerald green of grass, the burgeoning green
Of berry vine, the long-hued green of fir.

The summer fills the air with sun the whole day long.
The summer sun takes the day in its grip and holds it,
Squeezes it, drains from it the last sweet drop of
       light.

The summer sun is long upon the land
And in the early fall, the fog drifts in.

How many years, how many centuries, how many
          ages
Did the fog drift in from a western sea, did the rains
          fall,
Did the green spread, did the crystal sun burn down
Before man stepped here? Who knows? Who can
          count the stars?
Then the land lay quiet under the hand of God.

They came. When? Who knows? They came
From somewhere strange (or were they placed here
By the other hand of God, indigenous, native to the
          land
They would never serve, merely inhabit,
While time and another people spelled their doom,
A doom as inevitable and irrevocable as the winter
          rain).

They raised no cities, laid out no roads, turned up no
          earth
For seed, yoked no cattle. They took no land,
But dwelt upon it, taking from it their needs, giving it
Nothing for they had nothing to give.
Sometimes they burned the forests down.

How long did they stay, taking their small needs,
Giving the nothing they had to give? Who knows?
And still the fog drifted in from the sea,
The rains came, the spring green, and the long hot
sun   of summer.
And the people lived in the other hand of God.

Then came the new people—they of the white skin.
Now the years could be counted, the seasons tolled,
The times of fog on the mountains, and rain,
And sun. They came and measured the land
And marked its streams and gave it their names.

And they brought their names—LaCreole, Rickreall,
And Ellendale; Lewisville, Airlie and Pedee;
Salt Creek, Monmouth, and Well's Landing;
Suver, Bridgeport, and Falls City;
Independence, Salem and Dallas.

Cynthian, Cynthian. O, where have you gone
        Cynthian?
Where is Dixie? Where The Landing?
Where are all the names that sound with the quiet
        rush
Of deep water running? Where are the names
Of the Luckiamukes, the Killamooks, and Salishan?

The people came. They came walking dusty trails;
They came riding tired horse; they came
Prodding tired oxen yoked to tired wagons down
        dusty roads;
They came sailing great ships that stretched tall firs
Above massive decks, driven by a wind they could
        not tame.

They came and laid down foundations
And erected their houses, their stores, their grist
        mills.
They measured the land and gave it their names
And laid out their roads and marked their cities and
        towns.
And they made their laws.

"Fifty-Four, Forty or fight!" he said.
"Fifty-Four, Forty, or fight!"
They gave his name to the county and called it Polk;
They gave his partner's name to the city and called it
      Dallas.
Gone were the people whose voices sounded like
      water;
Gone was Cynthian.

They marked the boundaries on all four sides;
They made it a state and called it Oregon.
In the center of the great valley, the valley
      Willamette,
They laid out its capital and called it Salem.
They measured the land and laid their names upon it.

Academy Square was laid out twenty-four rods to a
      side
With a street eighty feet wide surrounding it.
On the north by the creek that was called a river,
They raised the Academy and enrolled fifty-seven.
On the east they raised a courthouse.

They put down their stores; they put down their
      schools;
They put down their churches. They put down their
      roots.
And having put their roots into the earth,
In the valley, they said, "This is our land,
This is our place, this is our manifest destiny."

Old John Waymire dug a mill race around the square
And they erected their factories: a grist mill
And a woolen mill, a foundry which they called
Machine and Locomotive works, and a tannery.
Then when the tall fir fell, they raised a sawmill.

And when they had founded the city,
When they had laid out the town,
They set down a post office for mail,
Laid out a road for iron rails,
And strung wire for the telephone.

D. J. Riley installed a dynamo
And lighted the streets by the power
From the water from the old mill race.
They graveled the streets and ordered the marshall,
"Arrest the first man driving faster than six miles an
        hour."

And that's how it was three score and eleven years
After the conception of the Republic.
The people came and came and came.
They measured the land and placed their names upon
        it
And called it their place, their land, their manifest
        destiny.

In the early fall, the fog drifts in from a western sea,
Climbs the shoulders of the mountains along the
        shore
And glides along the hills that border the valley
Then slides slowly out over the valley and covers the
        sun.

Now gone
the cold wind.

Long gone
the snow drift.

Bright hangs
the full moon.

Full sings
the lone bird.

Spring waits
the full bloom.

Ride a dark horse,
Grey horse beside.

Ride a dirt course,
Green course beside.

Ride a dark horse,
Gently hooves glide.

Ride a dark horse,
Stride upon stride.

Ride a grey horse,
Search for a bride.

Ride a grey horse
Far, far and wide.

Ride a grey horse,
Bride close beside.

Ride a grey horse,
In love close abide.

Ride a grey horse
O'er the wide countryside.

Ride a dark horse,
Lost is the bride.

Ride a night horse,
Pale moon beside.

Ride a dark horse,
Hell's gates open wide.

Ride a dark horse,
Grey horse beside.

XII

And now shall I write deathless prose
while dead roses lie along the garden path
in winter long turned to rain while no snow
flies through slowly moving air to
who knows where and why and what
because things move along so in a world
gone topsy-turvy and all that rot
though to tell the truth,
and why should I be telling the truth
now when I am but pecking away at nothing
but gibberish trying to make sense
from the dust-bin of my brain
and the dust blows away in the light wind
and doesn't even bother to settle
in the corners of my mind though
windsong be ever so sweet in the hours
just after dawn while the body
is still able to move along though strength
has gone to weakness
although there is still the ability
to move about in spite
of an uncooperative heart
that jiggles in ragtime
when it should waltz
about inside a body
growing less and less able
to do as it has been commanded to do.

If there be sand in my grits,
then I shall eat them anyway
because they were placed before me
in the fulness of time and I am to eat
of the fruit of the vine and tree and grass,
though grass itself is inedible

unless one is cow or horse or sheep
or other ruminating beast
though ruminating is something
the mind can do if one sets the mind
to waking thought in dim morning light
while the lamp remains unlit and the fire
does not glow though the smoke rises
through the chimney tops and drifts away
in slow moving air
that hovers over all
through morning and evening,
sometimes growing strong
and lifting leaves and drifting them
into streets to be mauled
by passing automobiles and busses
and skid beneath walking feet
if the weather be wet and the leaves freshly
driven.

XIII

The bird sat on the top
of the post pecking away
at tiny grubs, the offspring
of tiny insects that flew
through the air in endless numbers.
The bird would fly away
for a time, then return.

Gordian Knot sat beside the pool,
fountain stone splashing,
feeling the warmth of the morning
beginning to climb.

It had been a warm night,
uncomfortable for sleeping,
though I had kept the window
to my bedroom open
letting what cool breeze, slipping by, enter.

Still, the breeze wasn't enough
to cool the room for comfortable sleeping
and I was tired, infinitely tired.

Perhaps my heart will begin to flutter again.
I don't like the fluttering
but it is inescapable when it arrives.

I loved my gardening,
had built the pool with its fountain stone,
had built another pool
where the water flowed
from a raised mound of stone
and splashed into the lower pool

with a sound of water running
in a distant stream, except
it wasn't distant there at all,
just outside the window
and when the window was open,
the sound was close and fresh.

I loved that sound because
it made the world seem
as if it were open to the great blue sky
where the birds flew, where the bird
that had sat pecking away at grubs
on the post flew. Then the bird
was back again, pecking away
at the grubs.

The top of the post
had grown ragged with the pecking,
the smooth surface of the saw
that had cut it driven into gullies and ravines.
Strange to think of them as gullies and ravines
in such a short space,
but I would be out among the gullies and
ravines.

The bird finished its pecking
and dropped to the fountain stone.
It dipped its beak into the water
bursting upward from the stone,
then flipped a wing in the water,
turned and flipped the other wing
in the same manner. Lovely bird, it was.
All yellow bodied with black and silver
wings.
It had been a lovely thing
sitting there on the edge

of the stone dipping its beak
and fluttering its wings.
Good bird.
I thought to return to the house

I would go where waters flow
Down to a blue-green sea called Deirdre.
I would watch red-topped waves roll
Up black shore-sand and slip away again.

I would hear the sea-bird's cry
Blown through hollows wrought
By waves breaking where sand-stone cliffs
  stand.
What did they say of Dover?

Did the white cliffs hover over
Sea-washed boat and debris,
There where the war was raging?
I would go where the tall winds blow

To a mauve-clad mountain called Sierdre.
I would catch the fragrance of pine trees
Gliding across moss-carpeted stone.
I would feel chinquapin thorn grown

Tough in sun-scrabble ground
Where few rains fall.
What did they say of Hiroshima?
Did the flattened houses and spires

Rise again when the war was over
And the sirens blew no more?
I would go where the driven snow
Marches o'er a plain called Mierdre.

I would touch the grass grown tall
Billowing green, gold and gray.
I would taste the bread, now dry,
Crumbled into clabbered milk.

What did they say of Waterloo?
Did the plain roll on and on
In endless columns of troop and horse
That rolled and raged when brought together?

No! I have not gone to Deirdre, Seirdre, or
       Meirdre.
I have strayed far from strife, and life and
love   and laughter.
I have stayed aside from the tide and waited
       for here-after.
What waits me now? A solemn bow to life's
       last master.

Shall I someday dream again?
Ah! No. 'Tis eternity that intervenes
'Twixt dreams and me. But then,
Again, I gaze upon sunlit scenes

Of waving grass and clover
And walk beside a stream where lies therein
The green backed trout, cool water over
Moss grown stones and pebbles where the
       young have been.

What dream is this that I behold?
Does God Himself lie in quiet sleep
While through His mind unfolds
The universe and all that lies in darkest deep

Of empty, cold and endless space
Where e'en a man may chance to leave
Behind a tiny mark on the place
Where he has been—a mark that leaves
       behind his face.

XVI

This is the dry land, the dead land
    Where no waters flow.
No lilacs grow where no door yard goes
    To empty stair that nowhere climbs

To roam where no bell chimes.
    Wind blown sand drifts everywhere
O'er stone burned hot enough to bare
    The skin when touched by errant hand.

All about the drifting sand writes
    Mystery, romance and more.
I would walk the green land,
    Catch the fragrance of lilac in my
    hand

And carry it through a door
    And up a stair where lies a room
Where soft bell chimes. There I would
    Stay awhile, languorous with love's
    desire.

We would talk of things of no import
    Though hearts sing a song
Of love held now but someday gone.
    I would waste away the time,

Fingers in your hair,
    Soft and dark as raven's wing.
I would hear chime of bell
    And song of bird—Tee-Twit, Tee-
    Twit, Tee-Twoo.

But now I stand in drifting sand
    And see the stone grown hot
Under sun that beats
    The anvil flat and hard and thin.

31

Will I sleep again?
    Will I dream again?
Will I walk beside cool streams flowing
    Into tomorrow and tomorrow and
        tomorrow?

Can I touch your hand
    And feel cool wind blowing,
Making your dark hair drift—dark sand
    On a lonely shore?

XVII

Turns now my world downside up.
This evening will I sup
on clabbered milk and green cheese
with dried crusts and spiced teas.

There is no door in empty space.
No window opens there to grant grace
to fallen angels who tread
the ground where they will bed

when time has flown
where driven snow has blown
all trace of these once known faces
from heart's now open empty spaces.

XVIII

My dear man, I'd love you most
Did I not love another more.
You and I beheld a host
Who watched long with sore

Hearts, but eyes that seemed
Not to see at all. Shall they
Some day see the light that beams
Through branches green and gay?

Now he sleeps where we laid
Him away. Did he know Gethsemane
Before he found the price he paid
For obscure thought, unknown enmity?

I would watch as sunken sun
Spills incarnadine across the sky.
I would know what we have done
This wondrous day, you and I.

Was this a man, or simply something foul
To be expunged by any means we chose?
Somewhere grey wolves howl
Their lament. Somewhere a rose

Rises sweet from fair ground.
Atop some lofty Everest, drifting snow
Shuts out the sky but not the sound
Of that heart beating slow and slow.

Does one live after and reprise
What he has done in this life here
Below a sky filled with blue surprise
That we behold and then hold dear?

This day has come and gone.
The deed is done. Do we feel
Good now that we have done
Together and set the seal

On life and love and falling star?
Let Golgotha come another day!
Let us see it from afar
In glass closed room wherein he lay!

Let me be a fish, green-backed in cool stream.
Let me be a hawk with broken wing
That knows no longer the sun's gleam.
Should I find again a song to sing?

I walk alone among the trees.
I hear the humming of the bees.
I know the scent of salty seas.
Now God alone my heart sees.

Do fireflies flit at close of day
Where once we ran and laughed at play?

Does the river run along its way
The same as on that other day?

I've traveled past where fireflies played at
    eventide.
I've watched the water flow past the river
    side.

Still I know that love will abide
Somewhere beyond this sorrow deep inside.

I'll gather mountains, pile them high.
I'll cup seawater, cast it high.

I'll touch the trees as I walk by.
I'll shout the night hawk's evening cry.

How then can I presume
To walk again where shadows loom

Long and dark 'til evening's gloom
Brings out the stars in that great room

Where all who live stay awhile.
I touch a sea washed stone and smile

A bit. I'll go now another mile
Or two then walk the last-most aisle.

XX

There is no sound, save an engine's muffled
       groan,
To tell us we are earth-bound, though we
       would be more.
Does the night hawk soar there somewhere
       below?
Has the cricket yet begun his song?

Below lies a checkered land, bound hither and
       yon
By strips of trees, green between ground now
       fallow,
And fields ripe for harvest, golden squares
       and rectangles.
Why are there no circles, do you suppose?

Is it that men think in corners sharp, though
Perhaps, circles would more easily worked?
There are circles somewhere far away,
I am told. But they do not lie here.

The eastern sky darkens, though no star
       shines,
To a deep cobalt blue. Is it true that
       sometimes
At eventide, the land lies long and wide
In soft caress of now gone light?

Is it true that down there where people walk
        the earth,
Children run and laugh and chase the firefly
        along?
'Tis so, I've heard. I can see none of that from
        here,
High above the grasses waving, the trees
        swaying.

The horizon is round, though the earth seems
        flat—
An arc that goes on and on until the line is
        lost
In darkness where the light has slipped away.
The western sky burns gold and saffron and
        crimson,

The light burst up from the now sunk furnace
        of incredible sun.
There is light enough for us to turn again to
        earth
And earthly things. So we make a slow, slow
        turn and glide
Toward earth, the western light turning slowly
        to shadow.

"Landing is an easy thing," the pilot says.
"Nothing to it at all. Just a controlled crash
And then a slow roll until you stop.
That's all there is to it."

Now I remember how once in deep
        September,
I soared above earth, hawk, cricket and all
that   lies
Beneath a plane that soars the sky at eventide.
I shall not forget, for 'tis eternity.

XXI

forever on the edge of almost
    stale tea
        dry toast
dead leaves crumbled into never at all

sometime, somewhere, someone ever often
    drifts with tumbleweed
        wind blown sand
dunes that are not where love's heart lies
    dreaming

pale eyed avatar of isn't, wasn't, will not be
    driven water flows whither away
        just now the down wind
floats birdsongs into river run gone

down garden paths of foot worn stone
    worn foot
        sandals damp
with blood from some grief outflowing

into never was until the something
    came and
        love's lament
fled to heart's discontent of now our winter

Green grows the grass,
Yellow the rose.
Soft sighs the lass,
Thus love grows.

Clouds scud in wind
High overhead.
South fly the geese
Where autumn has led.

White lies the snow
Covering the dead—
Grasses, flowers, weeds—
And love's drifting ash

XXIII

Great green backed Fish—Why do you go gliding from this deep pool where willows dip their branches in water, going tip. tip, tip, tip, tippity tipping along?

You have your nose toward the rushing of the gap, crashing and splashing and tinkling and twinkling along.

I've seen others like you thrusting the gap—tails thrashing and smashing and splashing along—slap, slap, swoosh, swoosh. Then drift back again to lie again, try again. Flap, flap, swish, swish—shushing along.

I'd drop a line but there'd be no hook for I'd rather see you as you are—green-backed and still below the green water striking diamonds and sapphires and emeralds thrust back by the sun—sparkling, brightening, shining along.

I know you have a task to do somewhere beyond the gurgle and jumbly dash of white water bursting along.

It is a quiet murmur here, broken only by willow's "tip, tippity, tip, tippity, tip" and a swoosh, softly for the water flows quietly along.

Go! Green-backed fish where you must. I'd walk a mile and wait a while to see your dreams come true—"Tit willow, tit willow" sounds in the trees. There a bird is sitting, then flitting, then bursting a song. A dart to the water, a beak to the water, a wing in the water flowing along.

Do you hear them Green backed fish? The tip, tippity, tip, tip, tip, the splashing and dashing, your own slap, slap, swoosh, and the tit willow, tit willow and wing flit, flit? Perhaps you are just waiting or resting or gathering your thoughts before you go again to the gap, slapping and swooshing along.

I must go now for I have much to do and people to meet. But none, I am sure, will give me such pleasure as seeing you here, green-backed and deep with the willow's tip, tip and the bird's tit willow, the splash, gurgle and crash of white water. I'd rather be here with you, but I must be going along.

XXIV

The temperature is ninety-five.
The humidity is twenty.
        Why, then, does it seem so
much more intense, here where the
land lies long, wide, immensely flat.
        Do those green hills that cup
the valley up, filled as they are with
green of fir and oak while here is but
gray of sage, gray willow, where a
stream is flowing, and cottonwood?
The heat index is much the same.
The humidity likewise.
        Yet the sun burns down more
intensely here in this place that is
strange to me (though I would know
more of it and the little I know I
already love).
        Would pheasant succumb here
where sage hen thrives?
        Would the mule deer flee to
more sheltered climes while prong
horn lifts his head as if to say "Here I
stay! Be gone with you. Away!"
        The jackrabbit knows not the
green of fir and oak; the tree squirrel
is out of place where few trees rise to
fringe the skies.
        Yet, I am happy here though it
is strange to me and the firred hills of
valley fill my soul.
Come! Let us look up and see a star!

XXV

The hours move by slowly
When the heart is out of time.
Whether one be great or lowly,
He'll hear the clock's slow chime
And know the hours move slowly
When the heart is out of time.

Shall I find solace in a rock
Laid down to ease my head?
Shall I hear the goose in flock
Pass high in sky o'er head?
Do I hear the babbling water mark
This thing I've come to dread?

Aye! Each of these and more
Follow the clock's slow moving,
While I count the seconds by the score.
Though night's horses' feet are grooving
A dust-path by my door,
They'll not speed at all the clock's slow
     moving.

'Tis eternity I'm living. That, and nothing
     more.

XXVI

I am no Christ.
That I know.
But I'll pay the price
Regardless, then I'll go.

I cannot soothe your grief,
Try though I may.
May there come some day relief.
"Tis there," I've heard some say.

No. I am no Christ.
Though cross I'd bear,
If that were given me.
My Lord, I do not dare
To grant eternity.

XXVII

I walk alone through falling rain
That whispers love songs from afar
And hear the call come strong again
As if from yon falling star
Seen but briefly through distant
Broken cloud.

XXVIII

I'd walk among the stars,
Drink up the universe.
I'd walk along a flowing stream
And there I'd immerse

Myself in green, green grass
And thrust my soul in growing tree.
I'd listen as the living earth
Sings songs of joy to me.

I'd walk along the brow of hill
Where wind lays fingers
In my hair and draws
Me there where memory lingers.

I'd walk along a lighted street
And feel the presence of people there.
How now shall I rehearse
All this my heart to bear?

I'd do all this and more,
One moment to have again,
You in my arms
As in my heart you've always been.

There was a time when I heard laughter
Come quick from running brook.
My young man and I oft passed there
Where ran white frothy water and took
Our breath away. Above us rose no rafter.

There was a time when I walked the sun along
And heard a bird call to her mate.
I loved then and was loved by one
Who loved me too, and life was great,
Filled with wonder as it was, and the bird's
        sweet song.

There was a time when I plucked the lyre
And made music for dancing feet.
'Twas a time of joy when skies were blue
And soft white clouds chanced to meet
And touched and mingled 'bove yon temple
        spire.

There was a time, but it has fled
From sight and sound and touch.
The lark ne'er sings in this dark place
Nor violets bloom nor roses twine, for such
Is your will, my Lord. For this my heart bled.

I would walk again the garden path
And have my young man loose me.
I would gaze again a starry sky
With no moon shining. Ah, 'twould be
For me a willowed pool for cooling bath.

I would know again the warm sun shining.
I would know again the fire's glow.
I would know again the wild bird's call
And the sweet sound when the winds blow.
I would know again his arms 'round me
    twining.

But now they're gone while you play a game
Of wills, though in the earth I lie crying.
And somewhere out there 'neath clear blue
    sky
My young man waits though long I've been
    a'dying.
From where I lie, there's none but You to
    blame.

Damn your will, Sir! Damn your will!
Your cosmic game you have played
And now for me there is no place
Where my love would me have laid.
Your will be damned. The earth above is still.

XXX

Sang once the lark.
'Twill sing again some day.
Blossomed once the rose.
"'Twill bud and burst again," you say.

How loved the lark to sing and sing
And fill the sky with wonder.
How twined the rose along the ground
And spread fragrance broad as thunder.

Ne'er comes the day
When flitting lark shall cease to sing.
Nor comes the day when blossomed rose
Sweet scent will fail to bring.

XXXI

Once I longed for grace
That on some distant day
I would see Him face to face.
There's a greater price to pay

To gain that sweet repose.
And so I'll take a tiny place
Far apart from those
Who know their place

Is there and safely found.
For me, a corner far
From the table round
Beside a gleaming star,
There, I'll see Him from afar.

XXXII

When does love begin?
How does one know?
When and how does love end?
How does one know?

Did love begin with the sparkle
In your eyes, your hair,
Beneath a lamp or in the fire's glow?
Did I love even then?

The burning clock is lit.
Its yellow smoke curls thrice above the valley
     floor,
Disintegrates. Solitary dreams linger
In the scent of incense.
The hills rise up round in the evening sky;
Shadows linger, stretch their way
Across the red earth turning,
And shadows, stretching,
Lay their dark fingers over all
The soldiers, over all the young soldiers—
The living and the dead.

The waters of Babylon flow slowly by;
In the willows, the lyre strings hum
In passing wind.
"Who am I?" saith the Lord.
"I am the fire that through the green furze
Drives flower-bright. I am the fire
That levels mountains, builds cities,
The fire that turns the elements against
     themselves.
I am good. I am evil. *I exist!*"

XXXIV

We sip tea and speak of this and that.
Outside the garden flowers;
Below the park grows green with tree and
      grass.
Do we know the wind that passes there?
Do we know the bird's sweet song?

In another room others speak of this and that.
"Have you told him of your plans, Maki?"
The voice is vigorous, strong.
Why does it intrude upon our quiet talk?
This is his home where we sit.

"I would like to work on my doctorate," you
      say.
And you lift your eyes and look into mine.
"And where would you like to go?" I ask.
"To Oxford," you say, "but it is expensive,"
And you laugh in a quiet way.

You take photographs from a folder
And pass them on to me.
"This is my father, and this my mother,
This my aunt, my mother's sister."
Slender is your father, your mother too.

And we turn again to this and that,
Your eyes cast down, yet you know I am here.
Your voice is soft as the wind in night air
When stars shine and perhaps a moon.
And we are quiet then for a time.

Do you remember how it was, so long ago,
When you were student and I teacher
And on our last parting you asked,
"May I have a hug too?"
No. You will not remember
For many yesterdays have come and gone.

"Now, I must go," I say.
But it is not so.
I could stay a while.
But what would we do?
Speak more of this and that,
Sip more tea?

And so you walk me to the car
And I give you another hug.
"You will write?" you ask.
"I will write," I say.
And now you look into my eyes and there is
          more to say.
Will we speak again some day? If so, in what
          way?

I drive away,
You wave your hand.
Oh, I'd stay longer
But there are those who'd say
"He's daft, to look at her that way."
And so I go and you wave your hand.
So it is now between you and me.

XXXV

A man stepped up to the world one day
And said, "Well, here I am.
What are you going to do about it?"

And the world, impassive, said,
"Give you tasks worth a man's doing.
What are *you* going to do about them?"

And the man answering, said,
"I will accept the tasks, bear the burdens,
And endure. Is there a reward for that?"

And the world, unmoving, said,
"Your portion of joy, sorrow,
Ecstasy, agony, victory, defeat."

And the man said, "So be it."
And the world said,
"It is good. It is good. It is very good."

What was it Merlin said,
When he spoke in *Camelot*?
"I youthen. I do not grow old."
I would be so, yet

I feel in my bones
This growing older.
There was a time when
I felt always young—

That eternal sense of youth
That Merlin spoke.
They came to me the same each year.
Those young men, those young

Women, eyes gleaming clear.
Oh, yes. There were those
Whose eyes bespoke despair
And turned away in blank stare.

But they were few, grown old
Far beyond their time.
Most were young, eternally young.
How long is an eternity?

And does one end and another
Begin, I wonder.
Now I am come where
Walking is a chore

And voices are slow, uncertain
And ears are cupped to hear
Though words slip softy through the air.
And do I grow old

And slow, and speak in whispered tones?
It must be another eternity
Come to guide me along the way,
Though I too would youthen.

XXXVII

I know whose fields these are
That lie new-mown in late June
While the full moon walks
A starlit sky.

"Tis said greater stars lie
Beyond these my eye surveys.
My mind can understand that and more,
For 'tis bigger than that universe I gaze upon.

Still I wonder how God made the stars.
Did he paint them with a splatter
Brush on cobalt dome of sky?
Or are they tears divinely shook

From divine eyes that knew
The course of man's events
Not yet shaped by cosmic hand
From clay not brought by demand.

Yes. I know whose lands these are.
I see the fences in moon-glow
And star-shine too. I'd wait a while
If I could. But there are things

To do: poems to shape, perhaps a book.
Yet I'll take another look
At these lands now fenced around
By men who know how to fence

Things in, or out. I know
Not which he's about.
No one can fence the universe,
Nor frame God's plan in verse or book.

And so I take another look
And go my way 'til another night,
I, perhaps, may stop to look again
At lands that eons made

Before men fenced them in
For some reason neither they nor I
Can really understand as we
Understand the sky.

Lay down your burdens, Moses.
Come walk with me along desert sands
where lie bleached bones of camel,
sheep, man, where drifts the golden,
no, not golden but some insignificant odor
of withered grass turned straw
in some man's pasture where cattle
no longer roam, and climb with me
yonder mountain where the slope
lies deep 'neath hopeless, helpless vegetation
which will go on living simply because it can
and will and can and will endure and prevail
after man has thrust his last dying missile
into the air to fall who knows where
but all the while taking that which is human
with it leaving only this, the verdure
of the mountain slope where no man walks,
no cattle browse, no sheep ramble
though starshine gives way to always
trudging dawn drawn from once sunk sun
to high noon and dust parts the way
where our feet would not go
but must because sandaled feet
once walked a stone path to a Golgotha
that was false because man took the dream
of sacrifice and turned it into excuse
for demonizing himself and turning
the world topsy-turvy until there remained
only the lonely detritus of what had been
and may be again, should there be man still
      living
in the dead land in the ruined cities
in the devastated countryside where grass
still grows green in spring and trees

stand tall, sentinels against the burgeoning
light of dawn when there is no dawn at all
because to have a dawn, man must exist
to view it and sing aloud a song of beauty
risen from night's dark ashes.

I always knew Napoleon's daughter
Would never do just what she ought'er.
But Old Napoleon always thought her
The best the Lord his wife had brought her.

There was a twinkle in her eye
Even when the master would pass by.
She'd never moan or wail or sigh,
Just lift a brow, and let a smile lie

Where neither Napoleon nor the master
Would catch the smile any faster
Than they caught the fish they cast for.
She never thought to find disaster

As she whiled away the day
Atop some steep hill where on she lay
In grass and clover that would not pay
To reap and dry for winter's hay.

Yet Napoleon's daughter swept the floor
And shooed the chickens out the door
And had dinner ready when work was o'er.
Both thought her sweet to the core.

Yet, Napoleon's daughter slipped away,
Long after summer's close of day.
She'd go along another way
Where skies were blue, not gray.

Now Napoleon earns his keep
As of yore. And he'll reap
The hay 'til some deep
Shadow comes his soul to reap.

New Moon! You cast a glow
I'd never know,
Were I not aware that you cast
But shadow from the sun
Where it lies beyond our ken.

That haloed cup is swallowed up
In cobalt sky now filled with stars.
Starshine fills the land
As from dawn of time.
How dare the Sphinx ask the question:

"What walks thus and so?"
Rather pose the query:
"When and where does moon-glow
Come from darkened space
Where no stars show?"

Open wide the doors to mind
That understands but still seems blind
To universal truths that bind
The heart, the soul, the other kind
Of unknown thought left far behind

Dark moon in starlit sky,
Does the sun dare to die?

Soft in the night I lay all care away.
Night for a time will serve to stay
Day's harsh, hard reminder that dreams often
      flounder
On shoals and bars and drifts that rend
      asunder
The swiftest ship life e'er made for lad or
      maid.

Hush now! The night is coming soon,
Putting on stars and dangling a moon
And laying on the land a coverlet
Spun from gossamer and silver
Dropped down from dome of sky.

Poems in the night when I should be sleeping
Through my 'fuddled head come creeping.
Shall I turn them away and say,
"Come another time—when it is day!"

Nights are made for dreaming.
Nights are made for soothing seeming.
Poems should come by daylight
When all the world is touch and sound and
      sight.

Yet poems still come roaming
When the hour is far past gloaming.
I turn them not away, though I should say,
"Be gone! Away with you! Come in light of
      day!"

XLIII

No dreams come to beckon me.
'Tis more as if sleep fails to see
A proper time, a proper place
To wipe the sweat from my face.

Heat slides along the floor,
Touches walls, touches door.
A light breeze glides along the way,
Touches me, then slips away.

No! 'Tis no dream at all,
Nor does the heat leave the wall.
Is there a moon now, the sky to sail
And cause Coyote's yip, yip and wail?

Curtains close the world to me
Though God knows I'd like to be
Out there beneath a cobalt sky
Filled with stars, some flashing by.

But 'tis not to be
For sky too is closed to me
By low wayward cloud,
And, higher up, thin shroud

Closes off the universe .
How then shall I rehearse
The silent, sybilant song
Night has brought along.

I would be Coyote there
Raising voice in night air.
But even that is gone
For soon the rising sun

Shall grasp the land in warm embrace
And night shall turn away its face.
Why, My Lord, did you request
Fruit from budding tree?

Not even cherry could offer you
Fruited bough and not rue
The aftermath of all the pain
And sorrow laid out again.

Thus does tree shake my soul
And twist my mind and take its toll
Of word wonder in the night
When no dream comes, just the light.

I shall lay aside my pen
And lay my body down again.
No dream comes late this night;
I simply await the coming of the light.

XLIV

No fly buzzed when I died.
No footfalls slipped across the floor,
No voices whispered in the rooms,
No scent of flowers anywhere,
No taste of wine upon my tongue,
No satin lay beneath my head.

All these lie far behind,
Though some had thought them there.
The rooms are sterile,
Cleaned of all humanity.

I now have passed beyond all sense,
The living thought they knew,
Though passing there was fleet.

Now I know what they knew not:
Life is but a speck of dust
Upon eternity.

XLV

I never learned how to grieve
Nor even how to love,
Yet, I know what silence is
When house and heart are empty.

Though breezes by the house pass slow,
And birds have stopped their singing,
No bells within my heart are ringing,
and laughter, like the birds, is winging.

My Lord, I ask no relief from grief,
If that is what I'm feeling.
Grant instead Your grace to those
Who love and serve you better.

Only those deserve Your love
Who in their lives tender
All they have and do to You
That I have failed to render.

Ah, yes. 'Tis true. Each week I pass
Time with those who give their lives
To You in quiet solitude
And bow low to Savior's splendor.

But I have never learned to grieve,
Nor even how to love.
But I'd bear the cross if I could
For those whose hearts are aching.

I am not a poet!
No, don't argue with me!

I don't write a poem.
A poem writes me!

"Tis clear I'm no poet,
For a poem is free

From life's limitations
And wants me to see

What lies there (sighs there?)
Just waiting to be.

It's clear I'm no poet,
Nor want to be.

Come. Walk with me beside the river and sit beneath a tree with a cool breeze flowing by.

Perhaps in the river, a poem swims by and with good fortune we can hook it (not cook it) and see how it lies—iambic, trochaic or otherwise.

Perhaps in the tree there—high, high up near the sky—we will spy a poem perching and singing on bough in the wind. With light wings a-flutter and a tweedle-de-de, the poem may swoop down so we can see how it's shaped, how its song is to be.

Perhaps in the breeze a poem drifts by and still with good fortune and a net near at hand, we can catch it (not smash it) and see how it flies, in couplets or tercets or four footed quatrain.

No! I am no poet.
Am not likely to be.

A traveler on life's highway
With all its hump, fiddle-de
Is what I will be.

And if for a moment
I am fortunate enough,
I'll stumble on a poem
And it will catch me.

XLVII

The poet's song no longer lies upon the land.
The poet's song is but the muse of drifting
sand.

I bow before the wind that sends the grasses
waving;
I know the forlorn cry of lost souls' craving.

I scan the words lying here, flat upon the page
And feel a generation's lust and rage.

Why, then, can I not divine a truth in these
words
Lying bright upon the page, sans whey &
curds?

Milkweed withers, green gone, blown away
By sun-seared sky and sun-wind blowing all
to gray.

No fog comes to soothe land, now dry and
harsh.
Split-seamed residue of once teeming marsh

Lies dry and flat and hot. Though evening
come,
No cool breeze slips this way to sum

The digits or parse the syntax of war's
creation.
No poet's song has power enough to lave the
nation.

And as we dwell together here,
Though the pages cannot shed a tear

As did those thousand eyes and more
When planes incendiary flew the core

Of downtown Manhattan.
They will not wear silk or satin

To consecrate that hallowed ground
Where twin towers and more once were
            found.

No! Denim, duck or tweed will do
To honor those who served and those who do.

Lift the page; scan the page, feel the rage!
But the rage is gone, and someone sage

Has said, "It is done! It is done."
Let us heal the wounds and bring dead sons

Home and place them in the ground.
Let your voice whisper a soft sound,

And let the pages lie
Silent as words roll by.

XLVIII

I looked into a man's eyes.
Then I saw that he was naked.
I could not clothe him,
For he was proud,
Proud and bitter.

I looked into a man's eyes.
I saw that he was lonely.
I could not be a friend,
For he was proud,
Proud and bitter.

I looked into a man's eyes.
I saw he was afraid.
I could not give him hope
For he was proud,
Proud and bitter.

I looked into a child's eyes.
I saw that he was longing.
I knelt and touched him
For he was open.

When I looked again,
His eyes were shining,
For there was hope and he stood tall,
Tall and proud,
No bitterness at all.

XLIX

Those sonnets sent from Portugal
Ne'er sailed as high as yon seagull
Bending wing to strong salt breeze
Floating fixed o'er breaking seas.

I've heard the sonnets sung
These many years by old and young,
But their music seldom sounds
As sweet as sand sweeping yellow mounds.

Let them count the ways to love;
I'll count but once, and gaze above
Beyond the world I know,
At stars that march out, row on row.

I"ll ne'er forget the day we met.
Around my heart you cast a net
That would not break
For hurt or harm or other's sake.

I'll count the time I remember
How light fell softly that November
Eve while softly falling rain made damp
Your hair and hood beneath the lamp.

I"ll count the waves breaking, one by one,
'Neath skies of grey and covered sun.
I'll see waves roll the logs along
And slip away in silent song.

So let the sonnets move along,
For in their way, they too are strong.
But I will count but one, my love,
As Christ brought down but once the dove.

L

Moses never set foot here.
Jacob pillowed another stone.
Jesus carried his cross on stone
worn smooth by sandaled feet elsewhere.

I know not from where these glyphs came,
nor when.
Yet they lead me on to spirit greater than I,
And I stop and sit a while and think a bit
And feel something passing by that speaks

To me of that which is greater than ever I
Believed could come. Standing here, rimrock
     above
And bright green giant rye beyond, and
     beyond that
More rimrock yet, and sage and grass

Burned to sand color, I am drawn away
Beyond this place, up, down, out, away
Where some great spirit lies beyond
All else that I have known before.

I know I tread hallowed ground
And I am led to bow my head and pray.

LI

As we crush the marble pillars
of truths
now grown old, out of use,
their dust—
that residue of their existence
that we
cannot erase—burns our nostrils,
and blood
flows from new wounds ground
from old
hopes, dreams, and desires.

"How do I write a poem" he asked.
          "Do I take good words
and string them along in lines of
irregular length so there is a good
white space around?"

"No. No. No, that's not it at all."

"How then do I write a poem?
          Do I take words in lines
of irregular length and make them
march to a regular beat—dactylic,
iambic, trochee?

"No. No. No, that's not it all."

"How do I write a poem?
          Do I add internal,
external, masculine, feminine rhyme
after all those words march in
regulated time?"

"No. No. No, that's not it at all."

"You leave me bereft.
          How do I do it
anyway? Do I take a subject that
evokes a response—a sigh, a laugh, a
tear, a giggle or two?"

"No. No. No, it's nothing like that."

"How do I write a poem?
　　　　　Do I take those lines
　　　marching along to some observable beat,
　　　recognizable tune, then give it form—
　　　sapphic, villanelle, sonnet, ode?"

"No. No. No, that's not it yet, but I must
　　　admit you're moving along

"I'm getting along? If so, I rejoice! Now, tell
　　　me true how do I write a poem?
　　　　　Do I take an image or
　　　two, or three or four, and spread them
　　　around and give a nice sound?"

"No. No. No, that's not it at all."

　　　　　"Well, I've gone through my list
　　　and you've not helped me a bit. I give up.
　　　I'll never write a poem."

"Now you've got it! Hurrah!

You'll never write a poem. A poem writes itself.
　　　You don't do it at all. No more than a
　　　hammer drives a nail through the wall.
　　　You are but the instrument; you are the
　　　tool. You simply pick up the parts, sort
　　　them out and let them lie as they are.
　　　When that poem that was there all along
　　　takes root in your heart and grows tall fir
　　　trees in shimmering desert heat, you
　　　almost have it. When you have
　　　surrounded the poem, found its heart,
　　　corralled it, and loved it, and sung it a
　　　song, then opened the gates and turned to
　　　let it go, you have poetry.

"Are you a poet?" I heard him ask.
"No," I replied, knowing I had another task.

A poet takes words and makes reality
Of what to me is partiality.

Water in a well, a moon rising high,
Together, they make diamonds in the mind's
      eye.

Wind in trees softly sighing, bright song for
      lark
Make melodies, if he be fortunate, a poet's
      pen may mark.

I think I've not yet learned how 'tis the poet
      turns
Words to wonder while in the heart fire burns.

No. I've another task. Till the field, plant the
      seed
Wait long to harvest grain, yet reap the lowly
      weed.

LIV

Rabbit, you raise your ears
To sound, perhaps to sight—
For I am sure you see me here.
We love life whenever we can, you and I.

I'd think you'd dash away,
But you remain a moment
And, I suppose, wonder why
I stand and look at you.

I'll tell you true, my lad,
We love life whenever we can.
Those ears stand tall and still—
Are they from Midas come?

Ah, well. You've gone away.
Come again another day
And sit beside my shoulder
And whisper of things you know—

The sand, the sage, the grasses grown over.
Do you slip away when the moon is high?
Do you like the cool as much as I?
Rabbit, come walk with me!!

I know. I know! Our worlds are not the same.
But somehow I think we could
Commune for one small moment
For we love life whenever we can.

Morning's come again
And I am here.
Perhaps I'm where I should have been
Had I held life more than mere
Waiting for some quiet end.

Eternity lies somewhere there
Beyond a cobalt sky
Filled with stars no more rare
Than diamonds flashed from your eye.

LVI

Remember, if you will,
How we walked beneath green trees
And heard the river's roar.

Remember the blue, blue water,
White froth over
And the green rush or grass growing there.

Remember, too, the walk
Along the road, not highway at all,
Just a good road passing by.

Remember this and know that time
Cannot erase what we did there
In such small time and such great space.

LVII

REQUIEM

I saw him there, that son of mine,
Upon blue carpet standing.
His eye was bleak, his chin trembling.
"Mom's dead," I heard him say,

(Softly there along,
The floor, the walls,
The house were moving.
Did earth tremble too?)

But I was not believing.
"You pull my leg," I said
And smiled in quiet greeting.
"No. Mother's dead," my son said.

Green grows the grass,
Yellow the rose.
Soft sighs the lass,
And thus love grows.

His voice was soft and gentle.
There was no floor beneath my feet,
No ceiling over.
No walls kept the thunder out

That from the world was coming.
"We must go to Lebanon," he said.
"It's there she'll be ;
And Laurel there is waiting."

Strong and tall he tried to stand,
His hand upon my shoulder.
But I could feel the tremble there
And knew his heart was sundered

By news he'd rather not have passed
To one once held in wonder.
All things go away it seems
At times when, all about,

Life has stopped its moving.
Silently the wind slips by,
And engine's quietly running.
We speak of how the wheat has grown

And how the barley's rising.
We speak the words
And know the words
But they fail in their meaning.

For the only words that soar o'er all
Is "Mother's dead.
I know for those who called have said it's so."
"'Tis wrong," I said. We planned it all along.

Pension, house, everything
Were set for my demise ,
Your mother following after.
We planned that way

And yet this day
All has gone awry.
"I'm sorry, my son,
That I am here

And gone is your mother."
He spoke no word,
Nor looked around,
Just drove along with me beside,

While from the sky the sun was shining,
And along the way
Green fields lay
'Neath April sun—

Fecund, full with living.
"Lupine there," I said.
"Beside the road
Among the grass.

See it—purple, blue, white and shining."
"It's a lovely day,"
I heard him say,
Voice quiet, strong and true.

But 'twas not so,
That I knew,
Though earth lay
Warm and fruitful.

Time went by.
I know it did,
For the road behind was winding
Away, black ribbon fit for tying

Bands for arms and doors.
Perhaps it too was grieving.
Then the miles were gone,
The road gently winding

Through fields of green,
And sometimes trees along the way
Stood tall and broad
With limbs upward reaching

As if to pray, while within
I felt my heart still beating.
"Come this way,"
I heard her say.

"Your daughter's here awaiting."
Strange, I thought.
Not dressed in white
But I knew better.

White is gone and formal caps.
But what is this I'm thinking?
Then more were there,
Those who cared

And came along to still the weeping.
Then my daughter
Tall and strong
As the laurel tree

With branches gently swaying.
Bodies twined,
Arms 'round her tightly.
Did the earth quake then,

Or was it we two trembling?
She wept then,
This girl of mine.
Laurel was her name.

"I'm sorry, sir,"
The words quietly lay
In whitened corridor.
"We did the best we could,

But we could not revive her."
"Her last words were a prayer,"
My daughter said. "I thought
You'd like to know."

Perhaps it should be so,
But this I know—
All prayers for me are ended.
Send prayers where you may,

But say no prayer for me.
I live without a life
For that which was is ended.
"Tis finished now. Let it be!

Softly runs the tide along,
The river's edge a'greening,
Sun traces a blue, blue sky,
Below the birds are wheeling.

Soft twilight brings the cricket's cry,
The tree frog seems a'keening.
Tall stand the firs on yon hillside,
Wide spread the oaks in valley.

Days go by—summer, autumn, winter;
Spring comes again and flowers bloom;
Grass and sedge wave in wind
That o'er the land is passing

Clouds scud in wind
High overhead.
South fly the geese
Where autumn's led.

White lies the snow
Covering the dead—
Grasses, flowers, weeds—
And love's drifting ash.

Let us go now,
Though time has fled,
'Cross fields where clover
once raised its white head.

Let us cross yon hill together
As we oft did before
When the lark's song
Filled the air with melody.

Let us dance in the wind
With the rain in your hair
Softly shining in lamp's glow.
Let us walk where wild grasses grow..

Be still my heart, be still my soul,
For part of me is missing.
Ne'er again shall I walk with her
And her soft lips be kissing.

Blue, blue the river's rush, white water over. Green, Green the leaves, light breeze slipping through. There must be a where, when and why to it all but I do not know where, when or why. Yet I go on as the rush of river and flutter of green. Is that a train I hear in the distance? No! It is the river rush, the depth of roll and tumble and dash breaking together, folding together, driving together. Train of thought perhaps? I don't know. If there be train of thought it is lost in the jumble of senses that surround. Was that a black bird that flitted for a while near the rush or grass or whatever that grows beside the rush of water. Man has carved a niche in the side of the river. Laid a wall along and left a hard path beneath. Yet the green rush or grass or whatever grows there. And those who would have every green thing live into eternity would have no human hand touch the rush or grass or whatever. Shall I dance by moonlight? Will the moonlight filter through the green of tree? Will I catch the moonlight only from the diamonds cast back by the river's rushing? Ah, tis so. 'Tis so. I will come again some day and watch the river have its way. No deep pool here to open wide and fill with frothless blue. Water rushing to the sea over boulders and bars and whatever to make of the riverrun a maelstrom of churning frothing driving white water toward infinity for the river and its water flow are constant while time rushes by and I am no longer even a thought for I drive toward eternity and that hereafter that may be real or merely the hope of the teeming masses of humanity thinking, feeling, loving, hoping. All that jazz that men have thought over, fought over, sought after. How then may I know the river flow? How then may I know the drift of forever that lies out there somewhere without a thought or care for me in my small existence. Can I lay down words that will take me into forever? Not so, they tell me. Not so. I am earth bound and there is nothing that can hold back the night, hold back the star that flashes bright at eventide and comes to all.

I ride the dark horse, astride, the dark horse called eternity. It shall take me where I go, and so, I will not remain here where the water flow is a rush constant though the mind says all goes along. But still the riverrun changes not though none of it is ever the same. I shall join sometime, somewhere that jumble of riverrun and be one with the earth and sky and far reach of universe. I shall call a song, sad and joyous, beside the river and add my plaint to the sound of train driving into endless distance while time flows along, quite unbroken.

LIX

Be off! Shut thy mouth!
I'll hang before this man's breathing
Shall betray me with its stench.
I'll tell you how it was.

Beneath a coppered sky,
The smoke from yonder pipe
Turned down upon cobbled floor of streets
Where horses feet were grazing

Naught but fire struck by iron feet.
'Twas there none knew at all
Who knows not man nor maid
Upon the sward's greening

Beside a bush beyond a lamp
'Neath leaden sky
With no moon shining.
I have known it all, known it all already.

See! Beyond yon park,
Beyond yon streets and houses
Where near dead men lie breathing,
Sleeping lives away,

The river lies gleaming
Where lamps beside the waters streaming
Make it so.
There the river runs slowly.

Not rushed along with tide's ebbed flow,
Adrift with swill and sundry other things
Cast off by foul men's heaving.
Remember though, there is a place

Where clean waters flow
In chasms deep, through
Boulders, stones and flat of pebbled shore.
The bird calls there

And on the banks
The deer, the elk
Their tracks are leaving
Clean yet the water runs.

This I know for oft have I gone roving
In hill and glen and mountain side
Where waters go leaping
Down cliffs of stone, cool and clear.

But here beyond yon quay,
The waters are dark and gloomy.
One caught there a fish
Once a half-century ago,

Then cleaned it, cooked it
And set to eating the fish
Brought in from waters fouled
By men's dung and duff and other stuff.

Ere morning came, he was dead.
Dead from moaning and belly heaving.
He had fed from the fish
That came from the land of the dead

Or so 'tis said. I know it not
By seeing, but by hearing it
From those who've lived their lives
Away along this foul shore.

But I digress. I've to tell
My tale of woe.
For I loved a lass
And she loved me

And we tumbled beside the bush
Upon the green sward
Beneath a leaden sky
With no moon shining.

'Tis true, we gamboled there
And loved apace with
Such good grace, we thought
God would know our love

And grant us peace
When came the time
For his love
In greeting.

"We'll wed," I said,
"When I've come home,
For I must go a'roving.
"I'll be here," my lass said,

"When you've come home from roving."
"I'd not have it so," I said.
"I'd rather lie beside a hearth
With fire gently glowing,

And 'neath your head, a pillow
Spread for love's gentle flowing.
I'll come to you when I am through
With roving far and wide.

For there I'll make my fortune.
I'll return with gold doubloons
Enough for us to grow in.
I'll ply the sea trade

And when at last I'm laid
Back here where you lie waiting
I'll buy a gown, and a light crown
To grace your fair hair waving.

I'll buy and wear fair fancy
For your eyes to see,
And we shall stand before the Vicar there
And hand in hand be wed."

This I said and much much more,
For we were deeply loving.
And she took my hand and clasped
It close, her heart gently beating.

I'll ne'er forget the diamonds
Come from lamplight glowing
In eyes of blue, though dark night
Would stop its showing.

"I'll wait," she said, "I'll wait your coming.
For then we'll dwell far from here ,
This hell we'll not be knowing."
"'Tis this I wish, and not go roving.

I'd stay the while that we are one
And not stray far. I'll return again
And we'll be away from this foul place
And live in ways not known before.

We'll bear this short time
I go again a'roving."
I clasped her there
Upon the green sward

Beside the bush
The lamplight shining.
Then I kissed her hand,
Her hair, her eyes,

Her soft lips warm and winning.
Then I walked the mile,
The long long mile to where
The mast was standing.

Shut thy mouth. Still that fierce cackle.
I know 'tis true there is no grace
For him who leaves a lass behind
To go a'roving. But I roved not for myself

But the two of us and what comes after.
I know now, as I should have known,
That none can ken tomorrow.
But I live in despond depths

And deep deep sorrow.
So close thy mouth and let me tell
This tale of deepest woe.
There's none about who could shout

To heaven the anguish I bear
For having gone a'roving
When she lay in wait for me,
Hoping, hoping, hoping.

Ah, the ship, the lovely ship!
How fast it plowed the seas,
How wonderfully it turned to wind!
'Twas a wonder to behold,

Even from within. How wondrous
Must the gulls have thought,
If they thought at all,
For they were with us all the while at sea.

And we ranged far and wide
After the tide took us out to sea.
Many a land and many a sea
Did we visit and come to know.

Eighteen month, more than the year
I planned and said 'twould be.
But we crossed the Mid-Earth Sea
And found gold, diamonds, and perfumes

Fit for a king or a queen.
Ivory too we found, for carving
And for laying around.
Then on to the Carib seas.

There too we found riches
Beyond our imagining.
Took it all to the North Shore
of the Americas, and there

Traded for furs and maize
And good wool cloth
To carry along with us,
The good God alone to guide.

Turned round the dark sea under
Midst rain and wind and seas a'thunder.
Then gained we all the Islands
Pure waters and some loved

The sea nymphs flashing water
From long black hair. But not I.
I had a lass and would always pass
Temptation's slumbrous drift: desire.

Full eighteen month we roamed the seas,
No thought had I for none but she
Who lay in wait for me
As I knew it could only be.

Long nights I lay awake,
Thinking of my lass and the green sward
Where I loved her and she loved me
And all the world was a wonder.

Long I dallied on the prow
And watched the blue seas part
As our ship did dart
Upon the smooth, smooth sea.

I watched the dolphin glide there
And dive then rise above the blue-green
Waters flung aside by the ship's flying flume.
And when the winds arose, there was I

High in the rigging, laughing.
"Come winds, come rain,
Come blown spume from the sea!
To my love you take me,"

I cried. And shook my fist at the gale.
"I've gone a'roving and all's well
With me and my lass a'waiting."
I loved it then, the wild wild sea

And the blue blue sky,
And the gray cloud under,
And the creatures that flew the sky
And those that swam the waters.

They seemed to me to be my brothers
Or sisters or other, who would
Come with me and side with me
When my lass and I would wed.

Gathered I my riches too. Not a single
Farthing did I spend for pleasure,
But put all away that came my way
For that single wondrous day

When my lass and I, side by side,
Would lie far from the changing tide.
And when 'twas finished, that long long ride
Across tumultuous seas,

I came here and shucked my sea gear
And bought a gorgeous gown
For my lass and for me this
Fancy raiment.

One score doubloons had I then.
We'd spend it together
To buy a home and plot of land,
And keep the rest to make a nest

And turn the money over.
With what I gained, we'd live out our days
in quiet love and quiet splendor.
For such as we, a little would be

More than we could dream of.
Ah! Proud was I, to see the sky
And feel the land down under.
I laid away my treasure.

Ten gold doubloons I saved
For the glorious day when my lass and I
Would wed. But 'twas not to be,
For he came to me, that vile thing yonder.

Ah, yes! He came to me
And touched my coat, and gazed
Upon the ring I wore on my small finger,
A finger no larger than that of my lass

Where on the ring would lie.
Yes. He came to me and gave me word
Of how it was they had died,
First my father, then mother too,

Sent not to worms beneath the ground,
But to flames of pyre round
Because they too were bereft
Of life by a thing called "Black death."

He watched as I searched the rolls,
Even told me where they were burned
By committee set apart for such,
And gave me aid to read the names

Of mother, father, sister too.
There they lay, upon the page,
Just as he had said 'twould be.
And so the first great loss came to me.

Scarce three months since I
A'roving went, were they heaven sent,
For 'tis true that they, luckless yes,
But good and true to God above

And the Christ child too.
Though they be not laid underground,
I'm sure their names are scrolled
On great roll call for gentle souls.

But 'twas not the end,
Could not be. For I had spent
Too much time, wandering so
And gathering wealth and keeping

It just so, that when I returned
I might raise their lives a bit,
And mine and my lass's too.
'Twas too late, he told me

This "friend" of mine who bade
Me come to where they lay
Waiting for that day when they
Would be laid away in wormy ground.

Ah! I would have the keen ship drive
A homeward route swifter than
A gull's swift wing, for gulls
Not only sit upon the shrouds

Of ship but fly about,
Dipping wing to water and wind
And dart swiftly about the ship.
How good it would have been

To see the ship so move
That I could return to my love,
That lass who lay with me
Upon green sward, beside yon tree.

Again he aided me. He took me round
Where she was laid away, her babe beside,
Lost now to wind and sun and rain,
Though she would have gladly lain

Beside me and our babe in any
Weather, be it calm or storm.
Of this I'm sure, for she
Was bold and bright and lovely too.

Lovely she lay in coffin round
'Ere they placed her in the ground.
In all he guided me, to yard of graves
Where she'd be laid away

Among the potter's plots
For there was none to pay
The cost to lay away one who
Died, kinless and lost.

Tis said the last months she found
A place in brothel for her and our babe,
Though she lay with no man,
She made the beds and pitched the slops

And baked sweet bread for swains
Who pitched her coins, and asked her too
If she might lie upon the bed though unwed.
Always, 'tis said, did she refuse

Though money she would have
In plenty for her and our babe.
I would have wept if she had
Gone to bed with such as they

Though they plied their trade
With zest. This I know because of those
Who shipped with me upon the sea
And where we stopped, went to bed.

No. My lass kept herself for me,
And kept our babe, quietly
Waiting the time when I'd return
To take her to home and hearth.

But 'twas not to be. As yon man said to me,
"Your lass is dead as is your babe.
They lie in state in a brothel,
Waiting the potter's grave."

He took me there and watched my eye
As I gazed upon them where they lay
Side by side in coffin made
Of rough hewn boards for potter's grave.

The madam came and said she,
"She was a sweet child, your lass,
And sweeter was her babe.
She ne'er once betrayed

The love she held for her man
Whom she said would come some day
And free her from her bondage here.
But he came not while she lived.

Be not afraid that she lay down
With man or soiled her gown.
Full strong she worked all day long
At things the strumpets would not touch.

But she alone was true to love,
For loving can be true.
These six days has she lain just so.
No word came from kith nor kin

To make nice coffin to place her in."
Thus spoke the madam of that harsh place.
I looked upon her lying there,
And knelt and touched her golden hair,

And kissed the lips, once warm and true,
Now cold and hard, for the time had come
To lay her in the ground
With soft earth to cover her.

I took one doubloon and bought a coffin fair,
And chose a place on yon fair hill beside a
        tree,
Another doubloon they took from me.
All the while that foul man watching me.

He saw how it was with her and me,
My lass with our babe, now lying free
From all care and woe, from this world gone
To face Our Lord, as she deserved

For well Our Lord and me she served.
No condemnation could come there.
She would lie beside a star
Making heaven glow with light as fair

As that Our Lord will someday give
To all who've lived in love and faith
In all that he has taught to those who wait
For grace and quiet peace.

Now she is laid in the ground
And there is music all around
Sung by birds in trees with branches wound
With leaves of red and gold that make sound

As glorious as any angels could make,
For God, or Christ, or Mary's sake.
Think you I could do all this
If I had stolen raiment I wear,

Or the gold doubloon you found
Lying in state in wallet there.
Believe it not, for 'tis not true!
That man with churlish smile

Has led you all astray.
'Tis he you should assay,
For his word is as foul
As the clothes he wears.

Search where I tell you
And you will find nine gold doubloons,
All that is left of the treasure I thought
To bring my lass and father, mother,

Sister too. Took full half I had laid away
To put away my loved ones just as they
Deserved, sprightly and gay the world
Would be, for such as my lass, hair lightly
       curled.

See how he is clothed, in rags and tatters
And old cocked hat. Tis not I who has
Waylaid the truth. Do not believe a word I
       say,
But look there beneath the coat

He wears. Look beneath the coat at back,
Look beneath the rope that binds
His lackluster trousers to his waist
And you will find a fine soft purse

With nine fine gold doubloons hanging there,
A fine gold cord holds it hiding where
None should be finding what lies there
Beneath soiled cloth by soiled skin brought
       bare.

If what I say be not so,
Take me as you will.
For I have little left for which to live,
But to Our Lord and this world to give.

With my lass and our babe, I died
This once, though I remain open eyed.
My heart is made of lead which you may fire
And pour charge for yon musket

And aim well, for I too would
Go and live with my fair lass and our babe.
Place me 'neath the tree beside the wood
That lies on yonder hill.

If not, then bring to me that which he has
     taken
And let me go though quite forsaken
By God and Christ and fair Mary,
For I am as dead as lass and babe can be.

LX

I build sand castles formed from words.
I raise fine minarets, strong redoubts, tall
      towers and such.

Then comes the critic ocean waves
To wash them all away.

Then I am left with a plain of beach,
Long and fine beneath a gray, gray sky,

For the sun shines seldom on Oregon sand.
I watch the waves come one by one,

For such it is they come.
Each tolls the bell that calls for me.

The spring of life has come and gone,
The summer too.

The autumn leaves have fallen
And the winter snows as well.

Soon those snows shall drift away
And I wonder—Shall there remain

A part of me unwashed by critic waves?
Can it be that I could leave behind

A small bit of refuse
That some will recognize

As the residue of a soul
That lived and loved and wandered

Here upon an earth that holds
Not only fear and loneliness

But also love and truth as well.
I build sand castles word on word,

And wait as critic waves
Quietly wash them all away.

LXI

Softly sang the lark at sunrise.
It comes with some surprise
That I should now remember
How from bursting June to sere September
Softly sang the lark at sunrise.

How lonely were the lark's soft cries!
Why is it then I cannot devise
A quiet song that I could raise
To God in prayer and quiet praise
For larks that sang at morning's rise?

Time has gone but I remember
How from green June to dry September
Softly sang the lark at sunrise.
This I hold as one small prize.
But, O how chill the wind of deep December!

LXII

Where hast thou gone, silence?
To that shallow confirmation
of glazed clay holding flowers
or fruit as it may?

Hast thou turned to stone
that lies along the stream
and underground or
black and tarry along a road?

Go now, Silence! Let me hear
sweet wine from vibrant violin
wafted on breezes in soft eventide,
shining silver and gold.

Thou shalt come again, I know.
But for now let me live and love
and laugh a while before
I close my eyes one last time.

How can I forget Gethsemane?
Golgotha? Didst thou reign then—
Silence? Or wast thou buried in
stone worn smooth by sandaled feet?

Come, let me live again.
Let me sing again.
Let me sigh again.
Let me touch her hand

For lost am I
when my Gethsemane
moved on to Golgotha.
I am no Christ, I know!

But, thou, dear Silence
draw me now to some
stygian shore. I'd hear
her voice once more

If it could be so.
But now the room
is filled with thee.
I hear no fly buzz there.

LXIII

I build the wall, stone on stone.
Rough, sharp, even on gloved hand,
They lie quiescent where I lay them down.
Would they lie easier placed in sand?

What speaks this wall of stone?
Does it bemoan its fate, as if 'twere but a
        band
Of scree fallen from some lonely slope?
Or does it speak of something grand?

Some day, perhaps, I'll know this stone,
This ribbon laid upon the land,
But I think not, for stone is more
Than mind or bone can understand.

Will it lie here, this stone,
When I'm long gone, and wind has fanned
The grasses here, 'til rain shall come,
And sun shine down and I alone am banned?

This I know! The stones are sharp and rough;
My hands not tough enough
To make this wall seem like a bluff
Made piece by piece from such hard stuff.

No one grieves for summer leaves
That float green and rich and full against a
      blue, blue sky.
When apple, oak or viney maple weaves
Stately art on branches wide and high,

No one looks at summer leaves and believes
That some day they will drop and lie
Upon the ground and swirl round as sheaves
That farmers cut from fields and tie.

But thus it is when summer leaves.

LXV

Love is never temporary
As are phases of the moon.
Love is constant as the stars
That form a sort of spoon

To grace the northern sky
When clouds are out of town,
And the maple wears a yellow dress,
And scarlet is the sumac's gown.

Love is a steady flame
That glows within the hidden hearth
That lies within the sweet-most part
Of lives brought apart by softly mounded
                    earth.

Love is eternal as is the wind
That blows 'cross yonder hill
Where bird and chipmunk pluck
Sweet grains as they will.

Let the river's waters flow
Untethered down the stream
Where love lies dreaming,
A touch, a smile, an eye agleam.

No! Love is never temporary,
Nor will ever be,
For love is graceful, steady and reliable
As is the calm or sudden sea.

LXVI

There lies in each immortal soul
A twilight realm of consciousness,
A deep dark well to seethe and roll
With wild imagining and swift impression
Joy mingling with depression,
There to merge and blend by no fixed rules
In sleepy drench of forgetful pools.

No human eye can see them coil and turn,
No genius mind their destiny discern.
Yet all that each man is today
Or will ever be is here enshrined
And nothing else can point the way
But the deep dark well that is the mind.

O! subtle, murky, slumbrous thought
Of things that men so long have taught:
Of earth, river, sea and sky
Brought together in the deep will to lie
Unformed, unborn, till some moment's light
Shall bring them forth to mortal sight.

Here lies the truest heart—
No man can live apart
But must himself be duty bound
To find in tears a common ground
With all mankind.

Here lies the truest heart—
To stand in awe before great art
Or humbly kneel where trees abound
Among green hills that rise mound on mound
And dwarf mankind.

Here lies the truest heart—
Pierced often by the quick-barbed dart
Of loneliness yet strives to sound
The mellow note of forgiveness found
In all mankind.

Here lies the truest heart—
When other's sorrows, other's fears can start
Another flow, then this has bound
A gentle heart to those around
And all mankind.

Here lies the truest heart—
Humility is the beginning part
Which a bit of loneliness will pound
Within and bring the gentle heart ungowned
To all mankind.

LXVIII

Thus spoke Silence

"I am all.
I surround the universe.
I sing sad songs, glad songs
in silent hearts. Without
me, none exists. I am good;
I am evil. I exist
and may not be shut away
for all come to me some day,
even as thy love has come my way.
Thou wilt join with her
and me one day. Let not
sound lead thee astray. All
come to me on their last day"

LXIX

Tulip tops are showing,
The berry starts to sprout.
In evening, pale moon is gleaming;
I think I'll just stay out.

Willow down the river run free of all distemper from now to deep December. It will be a glowing ember across the floor of the universe where we may discern some fateful meaning of now and then and whenever.

All go forth or fifth or where or whenever because why is how to say nothing in endless drift of sound of sand under a column reaching to the sky but holding nothing up and holding nothing down, neither now nor then because all things pass away.

Even rolling Thunder's crashing roar diminishes the soul and all that lies within the whisper of violin and cello soothing as a timbered hill rising in deep green of fir and all that lies between on valley floor where doors don't open anymore because we no longer trust one another so we close the door keeping out intruder and friend alike, knowing not which is which, knowing only that late September moves quickly past October to lie with November and December.

All this and more lies open to the beguiling eye that leads on to a soft sigh of sybilant, silent syllable crying out grief and love and hope and loss never to return because there is but one direction in time's dimension and thus are all bereft of breeze blown through summer storm.

Let us go where we may.

From Earth we came, to earth we return and love it that way, knowing truth runs on to truth though we be unknowing.

'Twas on a day in deep December
When he rose from his bed
And looked out the window
At the tree standing there.
It stood bare then,
Devoid of all that made it tree,
Now a strange geometry
Against a gray, gray sky.

In spring it stood burgeoning
With new buds of leaf.
In summer it stood full and strong
With leaf that cast cool shade
Upon the ground,
Holding back the heat of sun.
In autumn the leaves turned yellow and
            scarlet,
Then fell in layers upon the ground.
There within it stood all hope,
All desire, all going to and coming from.

Let not your heart be troubled.
The tree is the source of all hope,
All desire, all forward thrusting ongoing acts
That lead to everywhere, nowhere, anywhere.

The scones are hot now.
The scones are hot.
When the scones are hot,
One must go to the kitchen and eat,
Though to eat is to live
And to continue to have hope,
To have desire, to have life.

And so one goes to the kitchen to eat.
After that one goes on about those things
That make life worthy even in deep
        December.

One can catch a wave roaming along a sandy
        beach,
A stream descending an ivy covered hillside
With sedge and grass and dying plants
Lying along the way.

One can walk the malls
And see old men sitting,
Twirling canes in dead hands,
Dead minds drifting toward eternity
For all leads to eternity eventually.

Is it true that the universe is a sphere
And that no matter how far one travels along
        its plane,
One returns to the beginning place?
If it is true that the universe is a sphere,
Could one travel infinitely
Around and around and around
As one winds yarn into a ball?

If it is thus, it would take eons upon eons,
Many more light years
Than were ever calculated, to traverse
Its infinite reaches.

A circle has no end, the song says.
Let the cherry bloom in spring time.
Let the apple drift soft blossom on the ground.
There is no loss of life as the apple blossom
        falls,

Only a growing of the applet,
Then the apple, then the ripening
Then the falling onto the ground,
Then the rotting,
Then the opening of the seed
And the rising of the shoot that could,
And would, were it not for all the other
            interferences
That occur in life, become a tree
Just like the one that now lies
Outside the window in deep December,
Its strange geometry traced against a gray,
            gray sky.

LXXI

Flowers of winter are few.
Earth is frost or snow, not dew.
While winter lies upon the land
Sorrow binds my heart with steel band.

Gone now is spring, summer, fall;
Gone now the sparrow's call;
Gone now the sunshine that filled my life
And laid away sorrow and strife.

Now nothing at all seems to matter,
Though sometimes rains against the window spatter
Or soft and slow and soundless falls the snow
And winter in my heart does grow.

Would I have it somehow other?
Gone wife, soul mate, children's mother.
And I alone my life and time will squander
As through this empty world I wander.

Will there be time, time to borrow
Wherein I find relief from sorrow
And turn my life again to wonder
That now has been torn full asunder?

Perhaps. But now winter's flowers
Are few, as are the bowers
Where birds of spring and summer call
And raise my head in love's deep thrall.

I think I shall not find spring again
Or summer's sun as it has been
So long within my life and heart,
For now my love has gone apart.

Now alone I wait for time
That I too that ladder climb
And join the universe and find the light
That filled my life and made it bright.

My Lord, I ask you not my soul to bless
Nor take away my deep distress.
I shall not come this way again
Where bright shining love has been.

My love is gone and I am bound
To this blue earth turning round.
And winter's flowers slowly grow
'Neath falling rain and soft white snow.

Now I walk the earth where sorrow grows.
Come spring I'll find a rose
Straight and tall from thornéd vine
And smell the earth and taste the wine.

LXXII

I hear the door bell ring.
I have heard it before & think
little of its ringing now.
I go to the door & there you stand,
A smile blooms across your wide lovely face
& there is a shine in your eyes.

Your face is not ebony, not ebony at all;
rather it is chestnut, deep brown with saffron tones
running through. Your eyes do not smile
as does your mouth. Rather, they shine
with loneliness & despair. Shall
I open the screen & let you into my heart?

"I'm Yolonda & I'm selling cleaner.
It's a good cleaner &
you will not be sorry you bought it."
I haven't bought anything yet, nor intend to.
Yet, you have a certain grace
that slips along my spine & I know I will buy
though I seldom do. It is your face & that stoic
something that rides your shoulders like a chameleon,

turning this color, then that, knowing all the while
there are few sales to bright young women with
all Africa bearing down on head, back & feet.
"I'm awfully tired. May I sit down," you ask &
without waiting do just that on the glider
there beside the door. The screen closes
& I, without thinking at all say, "Yes. Sit down
by all means, & I'll sit here beside you.
What is your name again? You spoke so rapidly
I did not catch it the first time."
"Yolonda," you say.
"Yolonda Herrington, & I'm selling
this cleaner that you can use for just about

anything you want." "Costs a fortune, I bet," I say
& you smile & say, "Yes. But you can't get it
in any store, just from me or one of the others
out there trying to sell. There are eight of us
& I am the only one who has made a sale
today. I've made four sales today & you
know what that stupid supervisor tries to tell
me? He comes down on me like hell won't ever
freeze because I'm supposed to be selling &
I've sold only four bottles. No one else sold any,
but he comes down on me like you know what."
"Sounds familiar," I say. "I have a grand-daughter
who was pulled into the same scheme in San Francisco
a couple years back. Promised her all kinds of
great rewards but wouldn't let her earn enough
to get home. My son had to drive down & get her."
But you aren't listening to me, not listening to me
at all, because you are caught in your own agony,

your own anger, your own despair. You don't
hear my words, yet yours keep flowing along
like the waters of a cool stream somewhere
trickling through boulders & small downed
trees that won't wash away until spring
freshet comes. "You have roses," you say.

"This cleaner is good for roses, for mildew.
Washes it right off. But you have to have
the right formula or you might kill the roses.
That rose there, the one at the end.
You should cut that rose half-way down.
It needs cutting." "No," I say. "I know roses.

If we had time we could go look at them
& I would show you where they have
new buds. They will blossom again within
a week. Not time to cut it now, even if it
does seem tall." You turn to other things.
"See here, You use this formula for this

job, & another for something else.
It's all right here on the bottle, &
this guide comes with it. Go by the formula
& you can't get it wrong. Why does
he do me that way? Tell me I got to go
out & sell even harder because the others

aren't selling at all. Why he come down
on me like that? You got a good name to call him,
a man like that who would swear & tell
me I got to do more because others are doing
less, nothing at all really? Do you tolerate
bad names, swearing & such as that?"

"Son-of-a-bitch seems about right," I say.
"Asshole," you say, & I guess you are right.
"I'm not really into swearing a lot, but sometimes
it seems about right," I say. "Well, he is an asshole
& I'll not say anything more 'bout that. I just
wish he wouldn't come down on me

When it's the others who aren't doing any selling?
Why they bring us here when they know there
won't be much selling? We were in Gresham
& Beaverton & we did fairly well there.
But there is just no selling here at all."

We sit quietly for a moment. The breeze pushes
through my hair, letting it blow about my face.
Hers is cut short & the wind moves it not at all,
but the wind is strong enough to move the collar
of her white suit-top. A strong breeze for
a summer afternoon. Should I remember

how it was to be young & desperate?
I was once, you know. There was a time
when all of life was spread out before me,
a vast panorama of doom. I had no hope then,
no direction, just a going on, putting one foot
before the other in slow measured tread.

My dear young lady, for lady you are, give
me your leaden heart, give me your doom,
let me carry them for you, though I cannot
carry a cross. "Come, let us go into
the house. I will buy one bottle &
wish it were more. But I want you

to know that I'm wreaking havoc on my bank
                account."
"Oh. I can't let you do that," you say & your eyes
say, "True!" I take my pen & write the check.
"In four more weeks, they have to give me
a way home whether I sell or not. St Louis.
I live in St. Louis & they bring me all the way

out here where I can't earn enough to pay
my way home. If I could only sell what they
promised I'd sell, I'd be going home now.
But that wouldn't work either, 'cause they
made us sign a six-week contract. You know
what that asshole gets. He gets a wage &

half my commission. Doesn't seem fair."
"It's illegal," I say. "It's called involuntary
servitude, & it's illegal in Oregon."
"But I come from St Louis & they
don't have a law there, do they?"
"I'd bet there is such a law there

but that doesn't matter. Unless you complain,
nothing would be done about it anyway.
How much do you earn, if I may ask?"
"Don't know, really. Asshole keeps the records
& we don't know how much we earn 'til
we're through with our sales & go home."

"Oregon law requires they pay you minimum
wage, $6.50 an hour, regardless of how you
earn your pay. Farm pickers in the fields are
paid by the pound for what they pick, but
it has to equal or exceed minimum wage.
You're in the same category. But you

have to make a claim." "Can't make a claim.
Asshole would give me the devil for something
like that. I'd never get back to St. Louis. Say,
why don't I stay here with you. I can cook &
I can clean house & I can help garden. You'd like
that, wouldn't you?" "Sounds intriguing,

but . . . ." "Well, I was just thinking how
I might get out of this selling something
nobody wants to buy." You sigh & settle
in your chair. I hand you the check,
you hand me the bottle. Multipurpose cleaner.
Good for all tasks. Wonder if it will ever be opened?

A dark brown-gray van cruises by. "Oh, there
they are. I've got to hurry. He'll be mad at me
for not selling two bottles. I sold four. We're
supposed to sell eight a day to make our way.
He'll be mad as hell I didn't get farther
than this." There is a smile in your eyes now.

I am happy about that. You have said all this
& more. You have moved me in ways
I have forgotten, laid away in some mind-
drawer not to be opened until my death.
Your chestnut face, your wide eyes,
your rich voice are with me. Be still!

LXXIII

You are gone they say, but
I know what they
Do not, and I know the song
That comes today
Through falling rain, and
With this joy
Find again when you were ever girl
And I but boy.

I sail the charted skies
Their wonders to unfold.
Once mysteries there I could behold,
But now I breathe with softened sighs

That so much is known of that
Which once seemed beyond man's ken.
I look the charts around, and then
Suddenly I know the cat

Knows far more than ever I
Will know of universe and God
And all that, It's odd,
I know, but now slip by

The wonders that are the stars,
The moon, the indigo blue,
That surrounds all the rue,
That surrounds like prison bars.

Falling rain, falling rain.
The hours slip by in falling rain.
Shall I come again while the rain falls
On rooftop and porch?
Aye!
I shall come again while the rain falls
on shrub, and tree and green green grass.
And the hills fill up with falling rain.
Why now the falling rain.
Winter comes with quick abandon. I know
The mountains are topped with snow and the
Passes lie deep and the trucks must
stop and lay on chains.
.

How then may I forget this day of falling
        rain?
Never anon shall I forget. For the rain will
Come again some day and I will think of long
Green summers and lazy days, if there are
        such.
So. Let it be a day of falling rain.
Let the hours slip by in falling rain.

Comes now the dawn and I am weary though I have slept the night through. There is dream there somewhere lying asleep behind a wind that slips around the house while the rain falls and falls and falls. There is no stopping the rain when it falls though there is a dry land, a dead land where wind blows sand across hills of sand building minute by minute and, should it have rain, could, perhaps, grow something other than more sand. But the rain falls here and not there, though all would have it otherwise. There is no stopping time nor the vagaries that come with it as the dreams of men flow like the river of sand that flows along. There is no living forever, though all would have it otherwise, there is no stretching into hereafter. Does eternity move in only one direction? Or would one, having slipped into forever, know the yesterdays as well as the tomorrows that lie there on the line of forever. Who would know forever even now? Not I. I have enough difficulty with today much less tomorrow and tomorrow and tomorrow. I shall digress and step away to a small stream flowing deep between banks of green grass, a full sun climbing the sky and all the generations of forever. Let the waters flow,. Let the land dwell with the wind and the small rain that falls there. I know. I know. There is no going backward into the joys that were. But I would go back nonetheless and see how it was when all the world was awake with living and loving and the sap rising in trees small and large reaching toward the life-giving sun. Ah! The sun. Let the sun shine down. Let the sun shine down. I would have the sun shining again though the rain falls from a gray, gray sky and fills the land with water sloshing about feet where they step. It is so. It is so. Let it be

LXXVII

How do you build a bridge when the river's
      rushing?
How do you climb a ridge when the winds are
      crushing?
Run, river run!
Blow breezes blow!

LXXVIII

Sorrow walks softly about the room,
And sleep evades me. Would I have
It otherwise? Aye. And it is so,
But I feel a sense of doom

Even in the quiet of the room.
Bring me willow bark to salve
The wounds that I may go
On weaving on life's taut loom

The sorrow that I must groom
As one grooms a horse to have
For riding in evening's glow
Though sorrow be waiting to come soon.

Lente, lente, currite noctis equi.
Sorrow rides the dark horse
And I behind must always be
Bound in time, the quiet course

That I can but resume,
Though I would find a quiet grave
Where I could lay me so,
And fill eternity's silent womb.

LXXIX

I climb the sky on road of stars
And there before me see eternity.
Shall I join those young men
Who spilled their blood on distant sand?

Shall I join my beloved who went first
When I had planned to walk before?
There lies Orion, bright belt shining,
And there Ursa Major.

Did they stand at honor as the young marched
      by?
Did they bow in salute as she smiled along the
      way?
Ah! Yes! Let me watch the world along.
I'll know some day how things lie

On this sweet earth, blood streaked,
Ash covered, yet lovely beyond belief.
See there the great blue seas.
See there the tallest trees.

I climb the sky on road of stars
And there before me see eternity.
Tis far and deep and soft.
I'll come some day. I'll come!

LXXX

Dreamers and lovers say
That nothing will ever pass away.

Yet, when day is done
And all they have begun

Has drifted to dust,
Or as iron, to rust,

They find that all passes
As the wind through dry grasses.

Those dreams they loved so much,
That love they sought so hard to touch

Are as tissue burned
With a flash and turned

To ash. So it is with all
Who seek dream's or love's call.

A morning will come when
Life has given warning, then

Dreams and love will be drawn
In ashes in the dawn.